ODE TO LIFE

ODE TO LIFE

Poems to Live By

Brenda J. Edwards

RESOURCE *Publications* • Eugene, Oregon

ODE TO LIFE
Poems to Live By

Resource Publications
An Imprint of Wipf and Stock Publishers
199 W. 8th Ave., Suite 3
Eugene, OR 97401

www.wipfandstock.com

PAPERBACK ISBN: 978-1-7252-8538-5
HARDCOVER ISBN: 978-1-7252-8539-2
EBOOK ISBN: 978-1-7252-8540-8

Manufactured in the U.S.A.   AUGUST 12, 2020

Dedicated to my father, John T. Brophil, for showing me how to live and how to love. I will never forget how you responded to Life's challenges, such as Mom's cancer diagnosis when I was eleven, losing Mom to cancer when I was fourteen, and then losing your job at Wisconsin Power and Light when I was fifteen. No fault of yours. And yet, suddenly, you had five children to raise on your own. And you did. Without complaint. Without support. Without notice. Each day blending into the next. But always positive when speaking. Always listening when spoken to. Dad, with few words you spoke so much because you spoke with the way you lived. I am honored and privileged to dedicate this book to you.

CONTENTS

Greetings, and thank you for reading *Ode to Life: Poems to Live By*. At the time of writing this, I am thirty-six years old and still trying to figure out my Life's purpose. For example, I am currently working as a teacher, attorney (estate law and contracts), and broker/realtor. I wonder sometimes how I ended up at this point, but I have no regrets. You see, I never strived to be noticeable, and I didn't have such grand dreams, either. I didn't even consider college, writing my high school senior paper about why young men and women should join the military instead. And that was my life goal: to join the military. I worked hard to train for it, running and with sit-ups, like a machine. Unfortunately, I get migraines and learned at Fairchild Air Force Base in Spokane, Washington, during screening (March of my senior year of high school, by the way), that that was the end of my journey. I got letters of recommendation from my employer to demonstrate my work ethic. I had report cards to show my work ethic as well. I pleaded over the phone. How could I be turned down so easily? Yet I was. And so, college was my only option. My father worked overtime to pay for it, and I am so thankful. I sat in the front row as straight as I could because this was it, this was my shot, and I did not want to risk anything. I wanted to see everything the professor was both doing and writing. And that was when I learned I could do it. I graduated in three years and began teaching. I am still teaching. I love teaching. But I also love to learn. I crave it. And I am still learning to this day. However, what I've learned to be most substantive in life cannot be taught in school. It is taught by living it. By experiencing it. By being knocked down, getting up, and trying again. By being human, accepting humanity, and yet challenging humanity at the same time. That is what this book is about. It is about humanity as we experience it throughout life. The good and the bad. I am hoping some of these poems will bring peace to you as I have learned to find peace with my life. For if a verse changes one perspective, one person, one heart, one life, I cannot even describe the joy that will bring to me. And that, I believe, is my Life's purpose. My father changed my world with his actions. I hope to change one life with my words.

LOVE

What joy! What youthful bliss!
Torrents crash my heart.
Yet, forceful hurricanes
each day when we must part.

My mind, I cannot think!
It is drawn to you:
The object of my being,
my clarity, your truth.

Do not jest! My spirit
cannot bear this weight.
Instead remain forever,
joined in joyous state.

INVERSE EMOTIONS

The lamp turns me on
to revel in the dark.
The door opens me
for a pathway to the heart.

The music pushes play
to hear melodic song.
I cover the house,
giving protection.

The water slowly drinks me
to quench a famished thirst.
You, my Love, a riddle,
my end and then my first.

PARALLEL LINES

Infinity. Forever.
Direction, sternéd way.
Stays the course. Does not turn.
Alone in all its days.

The other also rules
across the plane, so vast!
Unyielding in direction.
With purpose at its mast.

Parallel in time.
Parallel in space.
Lo! We've crossed each other.
Physics now erased.

PROMISE

The band: Eternal, mine,
simple in its glow,
quietly proclaims,
a love that we both know.

The band: Eternal, mine,
and yet it is yours too:
A promise from my soul,
depths of purity, to you.

And look! There on your hand,
a promise unto me:
Forever we shall join,
in eternity.

THE DAY

Flutters in my heart.
Flowing white in purity.
Groomsman by my side.
Can this really be?

Flowers and sweet maidens
and our families adore.
Vows creating union.
Who could love you more?

For if the flowers hanging,
and ornaments were removed,
remaining is the truth:
That I love you, and I do.

GIFT

A miracle has happened.
A different kind of love.
Improbable existence,
gifted from Above.

To cherish and to hold,
to carry and to feel.
From worrisome impressions
to joyous upheavals.

To share this with another,
or to keep unto my own.
Yes, a heart beating of Life,
a beating, not my own.

BORN

Five fingers and five toes.
A cry pierces the air.
It meets my face of tears,
of love, of all that's there.

Five fingers and five toes.
Perfection in my midst.
The blessedness is blinding:
Here's Life's greatest gift.

Five fingers and five toes.
Amazing grace surrounds.
Each breath. Each look. Each heartbeat.
This is the sweetest Sound.

HOLDING

Holding my sweet babe.
Gazing in his eyes.
Rocking gently now
with the lullabies.

He sleeps. I gently place him
in the crib, a blanket near.
I then continue working,
at peace with my Life here.

For when his dreams awaken,
and he looks around this world.
It's time to hold my sweet babe.
And, a secret I do know:

When others urge to let him be,
to cry himself to sleep,
the comfort from his mother's arms,
built strength you cannot see.

LESSONS

When blessed with my child,
my focus in Life changed.
My first occupation
was to wisely raise

him to know Love, to know Life,
to know Wrong.
To think before he acts.
To consider everyone.

Spending time with him,
at the park with basketball,
walking to the store,
I give him my all.

And I take away.
Boundaries are taught.
Love is tempered Time,
tempered Life and tempered Thought.

DADA

"Dada," speaks our toddler,
and he points in innocence.
"I follow you," and so he does,
stumbling in his steps.

"Dada," speaks our toddler,
"Dada, wait for me!"
His earnestness inspiring,
his want for you to see.

To see that he is like you,
that he follows in your steps.
His arms open wide, he smiles,
"I love you this much."

And when you scoop our child,
and hold him in your arms;
when you answer back,
"I love you too, dear one,"

my eyes tear and my heart warms:
A father and his son.
Nothing can replace this.
Not me. Not anyone.

CHILD

Innocence untarnished.
Windswept every way.
Joyous, angered teardrops:
Chalice filled each day.

Seasons batter greatly,
sometimes torn in two,
sometimes shaken down:
Refining perfect fruit.

Sweetness not yet tasted,
your spirit, youthful age.
Dear Child, you are free.
Free to choose your way.

CHOICE

Wearied weight I feel.
I weep Uncertainty.
Walls absorb the shouting.
I am drowning in this Sea.

Do I reach out for the timber
unfettered in its way?
Rebuilding former Life
to stay this course each day?

Or do I turn around,
face the vastness, leave this Sea,
reach out in hopes of grasping
a new reality?

MOTHER

"Mother," I do weep,
"I don't know what to do!
There was yelling, and I left,
and I came here straight to you."

Mother met my eyes,
waiting. Waiting still.
Deep breaths filled the silence.
Confusion over will.

I could hear the embers crackle.
My heartbeat slowed in time.
Mother waited patiently;
then her hands were holding mine.

"Dear child, were you struck?
Or did he find another fruit?"
"No, it is not that," I shared,
"It's just that everything I do

is wrong and he is right.
Nothing's good enough.
The visage that I loved
is now markedly Disgust."

Mother listened quietly
as my trivialities were laid,
nodding in agreement
as my case was made.

But then spoke directly,
sharply, and the sting!
"I disagree," she spoke.
"You should not be leaving him."

"Marriage is not easy.
It's for better or for worse.
My child, give and take,
but give more to make this work."

"For it does not matter whom you find:
Another with joyous bliss,
will fade to duty owed.
That is love. It's this."

I wept Anger and Confusion,
and did not know what to do.
So I returned to my dwelling,
and took each day anew.

And with each flippant comment,
and with perspective framing time,
I learned to laugh of trivialities,
shake my head, and sigh.

And now, my children grown,
I am so glad I did
stay and work and laugh
and love. For because of this,

given time, a breath, a smile,
they saw what Love can be.
They saw nurtured dissonance
become a splendid symphony.

TO ERR

To err is part of Life,
woven in humanity.
Forgetting someone's birthday
or the sugar in one's tea.

To utter in emotion
words regrettable, at least.
To act in heated postures,
unrestrained, a beast.

Worst yet, to act in passionate
conviction, angered flame.
Nothing saved: emptiness,
when the burning wanes.

Yes, to err is part of Life.
Part of humanity.
Balanced contemplation.
But imbalanced must it be.

FORGIVE

The yearnings of the flesh,
the body, and the mind.
Thoughts born into gestures,
then to touch. In time,

swords are in my back
and my heart has no more beat.
Anger manifests
as cruel and vicious speech.

But cease! Refrain and pause.
Was it flesh and flesh alone?
Can reason and forgiveness
mend the harm that's done?

RUMORS

Rumors circulating.
Gossiping is near.
Small towns and in cities,
cutting down with shears.

To listen or ignore?
To rebuke or reclaim?
Why does my mind persist
to engage this Game?

For rumors circulating
is idleness in tongues.
Speak and do correctly,
act in love and none

of these trivialities will
measure in the end.
For there's a much-more deserved devotion,
and to this I tend.

TEMPERED

It was during lunch break,
at a table with us five.
A newspaper lay unread,
but words were quite alive.

"Did you hear about. . .?" this,
and "Did you know that?" too.
. . . Dare I read the paper, dare I speak.
What do I do?

So as not to appear petulant
or as if thoughts were not known,
I nodded in sincerity,
though my conscience told me no.

Some knowledge in my mind
would have shaded all that's said.
But I withheld this urge to speak.
Lo, this burning urge was shed

with a politely placed suggestion,
a question of a sort,
to drift the conversation
to where I could comport.

And for that I am grateful.
For words when they are known,
are intractable in time
and no longer are my own.

THANKFULNESS

A glass full of clean water.
A roof over my head.
A meal when we are famished.
At night there is a bed.

A doctor can be found
when fevers strike its hosts.
When others have no help,
there is help for us, for most.

Why do I deserve this?
Why here with such a life?
I do not know the answer.
I pray thankfulness each night.

GIVE

Pajamas now too small,
or sweaters never worn.
Shoes that were too tight;
white laces still adorn.

Cans of corn and tuna,
peanut butter jars.
Loaves of bread. Please share.
Lifelines all these are.

HELP

The clock was quickly ticking.
Time was a thief that day.
I kissed my son goodbye
and went on my way.

Alas, if I were late,
abruptly would Life end:
No job, no food, no housing.
Homelessness, again.

But there! My dear, old neighbor
crouched in pain I see.
I call for help and rise,
but no, I cannot leave.

I stay to comfort and to calm,
as her eyes do close.
I lost my neighbor and my job.
But compassion frees my soul.

FUTURE

An alarm awakens me,
although my body slowly treads.
Sometimes I ponder this Day's purpose.
Sometimes no thought instead.

Difficulties will surprise.
Yet, rise and greet each Day:
An Opportunity, a Blessing.
Maintain your grasp and stay.

For to rest is quite enticing,
as are doubting thoughts.
But rise to become something.
Leave the world your touch.

LISTEN

Inversions. Dancing.
Unique and fleeting ways.
Numbers and words,
alive. Besiege the day.

Wandering throughout,
the title, index, page.
Eternal wisdom, hidden.
Why, oh why! O Sage?

"Hear and you shall see,"
Sage gracefully thundered.
I closed my eyes. I listened.
Epitome unearthed.

Striking knowledge. Here.
Quickly turn the page.
Wisdom's voice created
yet another Sage.

TALENT

A hammer on the house,
or lifting of my car.
Growing gardens here
or fishing from afar.

An office-laden day,
or instructing pupils new.
A caretaker at home;
What is it that you do?

For without your talent
I would be lacking very much.
I can't do what you do.
I need your gifted touch.

So continue writing stories,
with inventing, selling homes.
Continue doing what you do:
Your talents make us whole.

MONEY

Money, yes we need it.
For rent, for food, for bills.
But why does money rest
so high upon the hill?

Why does money shine
and glisten above all?
Why is it such a prize
when for it we aptly fall?

Because when we seek its visage,
where is family, where is Life?
What do our attentions yield,
but bitterness and strife?

For when money is attained,
it feels not, and you need more.
Money, yes important.
But consider cost, I do implore.

MUSIC

Whether country lyrics
or a rapping scheme,
Soft rock. Hard rock. All rock.
Puts me in a dream.

Classical piano,
or full symphonic band.
Music weaves a world
together with its hand.

FAMILY

Large eyes gazing, sparkling.
Tail wags at the door.
Quick steps all around me,
excitement bursting forth.

This innocence, protection,
this love without constraint:
This is endearéd family,
blessing me this day.

THANK YOU

I notice dishes in the sink
have been washed and put away.
The hamper is now empty
and our clothes are neatly laid.

I hear sizzling in pans
and breathe in delicious smells.
You help our child with homework,
help but do not tell.

The vacuum bag is empty
and the mop is now refilled.
There is quiet contemplation
in our sharéd world.

For you, so mesmerizing,
in your kindness, acts of love:
I thank the Heavens for you,
my angel from above.

LOSS

Cells that multiplied,
but they did not belong.
Or a sudden crash,
stealing Life too young.

Then knowing that this is
a new reality.
Knowing and then struggling,
fighting just to breathe.

A sharp pain stabbing deeply,
pulsing with my heart.
Years pass; I fully see you.
We shall never part.

STILL

Breath. Crystals.
Decorating air.
Inhale, exhale.
Climbing. Almost there.

Blissful. Agony.
Blooming doubts inside.
Mindful embodiment
pushes forward strides.

Eternity in moments.
Majestically endured.
Enjoy this saturation.
Life has met you here.

TIME

I have lived my seasons,
from youth to a sage.
My body seeks out rest,
my mind ready for this page.

When Time turns it for me,
remember what I've done.
Remember what I've foretold
of Life's joys and Life's lessons.

For seasons quickly pass.
Each day gone is a day lost,
or it could be a day gained
if you do what's right and just.

www.ingramcontent.com/pod-product-compliance
Lightning Source LLC
Chambersburg PA
CBHW051050030426
42339CB00006B/280